I0886628

WELCOME TO THE CONSTRUCTION SITE

# Bulldozer

Samantha Bell

Published in the United States of America
by Cherry Lake Publishing
Ann Arbor, Michigan
www.cherrylakepublishing.com

Content Adviser: Louis Teel, Professor of Heavy Equipment Operating, Central Arizona College
Reading Adviser: Cecilia Minden, PhD, Literacy expert and children's author

Photo Credits: ©Ostariyanov / Shutterstock, cover, 2; ©Bildagentur Zoonar GmbH / Shutterstock, 4; ©Ingram Publishing / Thinkstock, 6; ©SERGEI PRIMAKOV / Shutterstock, 8; ©Yevhen Anistrat / Shutterstock, 10; ©i-Stockr / Thinkstock, 12; ©Bannafarsai_Stock / Shutterstock, 14; ©joeygil / Thinkstock, 16; ©Jupiterimages / Thinkstock, 18; ©Westermak / Shutterstock, 20

Copyright ©2019 by Cherry Lake Publishing
All rights reserved. No part of this book may be reproduced or utilized in any form or by any means without written permission from the publisher.

Library of Congress Cataloging-in-Publication Data has been filed and is available at catalog.loc.gov

Cherry Lake Publishing would like to acknowledge the work of The Partnership for 21st Century Learning. Please visit *www.p21.org* for more information.

Printed in the United States of America
Corporate Graphics

# Table of Contents

Where else can you find blades?

# Clearing the Way

A bulldozer is a large tractor. It has a metal **blade**. The blade is made for pushing.

Bulldozers move heavy loads.

They push down trees. They push dirt. They clear away **rubble**.

# Different Blades for Different Jobs

Some have curved blades. They can carry dirt, rocks, sand, or coal.

Some bulldozers have straight blades. These are called S blades. They are used for hard or **compact** things on the ground. They pack down soil.

The **operator** sits in the cab. The operator raises the blade up and down.

# Extra Tools

Many bulldozers have a ripper in the back. The ripper breaks up the ground.

## Why don’t bulldozers use tires?

Most bulldozers move on **tracks**.
The tracks can go on soft ground.
They have strong **traction**.

# Unstoppable!

Bulldozers can move through almost anything!

# Find Out More

**Book**

Perritano, John. *Construction Machines*. New York: Gareth Stevens Publishing, 2014.

**Website**

The Great Picture Book of Construction Equipment
www.kenkenkikki.jp/pbe/push/push_003.html
Learn more about bulldozers at this site.

# Glossary

**blade** (BLADE) the flat, sharp-edged part of a tool
**compact** (KAHM-pakt) closely or firmly packed together
**operator** (AH-puh-ray-tur) someone who works a machine
**rubble** (RUHB-uhl) broken pieces of stone, brick, or concrete from buildings that have fallen
**tracks** (TRAKS) the metal or rubber belts on a vehicle that make it move
**traction** (TRAK-shuhn) the force that causes a moving thing to grip a surface

# Home and School Connection

Use this list of words from the book to help your child become a better reader. Word games and writing activities can help beginning readers reinforce literacy skills.

a
almost
and
anything
are
back
blade
blades
breaks
bulldozer
cab
can
carry
clear
coal
compact
curved
dirt
down
for
go
ground
hard
has
have
heavy
in
it
large
loads
made
metal
move
on
operator
or
push
pushing
raises
ripper
rocks
rubble
sand
sits
soft
soil
straight
strong
the
they
things
through
tracks
traction
tractor
trees
up
used

# Index



# About the Author

Samantha Bell has written and illustrated over 60 books for children. She lives in South Carolina with her family and pets.